Life

Love

&

War

A Personal Portrait
Through My Words

Custodio Gomes

I want to thank God for my endless blessings
and for giving me the opportunity to have the world hear my voice.

This book is dedicated to my daily inspiration…**YOU**

Life

Many see the strong front
that I have put up
But my heart has shattered
to many pieces
and many are still unfound
Life has been a struggle
beyond any visualization
I have cried as a young man
and as a grown man
But yet I still smile
to keep from crying
I have had dark days
and doomed nights
Yet I awake to simple
prayers and dim lights
Life has scarred me
and dragged me through
the dirtiest grounds
Yet I rise and breathe
because my blessings in life
have also been endless…

Complete Human Being

Aspire to become a
complete human being
Begin by speaking
out against injustice,
homophobia, racism
& gender inequality
Continue by sharing
your struggle, so others
can see the beauty of
being an inspiration
You never know who needs
to hear your story
End by being yourself...
God shines through you,
so don't be afraid of showing
the world your heart!

Seasons

Sometimes we fool ourselves
and pretend to live joyful lives
and peaceful days
But in actuality, we cry within
and hurt for the simplest things
For we seek all that was promised to us
in the creation of these worldly infatuations
But nothing in this world matters,
if we do not have anyone to share it with
See, this is what life is about,
laughing, dancing, and loving one
who resembles our inner dreams
But it seems that the trials
that we encounter, whether they be
within or without,
they come to strengthen our spirits and
to assure our hearts
that all things are for their due seasons
Remember that things do not last forever,
whether they are pains or pleasures…

Try

Dreams defer through lack
of consistency and fly away to never
be heard of again
My people have become accustomed
to accept their "fate"
So the hopes of becoming
a doctor, lawyer, professor, actor,
pastor…remain just
what they are…HOPES
We often see our dreams as distant
visions, that never evolve
into our God given talents
So we embrace the ignorance
of being "hood" and continually watch
portraits of success,
but only through a watchful eye
Rather than chase
our child like dreams,
we become complacent
Accepting of what could-have been,
instead of what should-be
Living our lives through images,
rather than our promised realities
So with humility in my heart,
peace in my mind
and a joy in my face,
I say to you, my people:
just TRY…

Before "an" After

Before we were blueprinted in His perfection
Before languages separated
our tongues from each other's love
Before religion destroyed
the unity of humanity
Before there was any civil war or world war,
before race, gender and color barriers
Before scriptures and eloquent speeches
made us separatists, imperialists,
capitalists and communists
Before guns, nuclear bombs, leaders,
dictators, super powers,
prime ministers and presidents
Before cars, flat screen TVs,
the internet and fancy cell phones
Before we learned how to iron-out our
conscience, manipulate our emotions,
and perfect our selfish desires
Before we forgot to love one another,
and before getting married for just a wedding,
and measured our vows on a ring size
Before we lost our faith
and killed in the name of democracy or theocracy
Before we stopped believing
in the Creator who believed in us
Before we finally realize
that He was before…there may
not be an after!

Changes

I've realized...not everyone is going
to make the cut in my future
I've realized that distractions come and go,
just to tempt and build my patience
Everyday is a struggle to
remain focused and it gets harder
It's frustrating to work so much,
attain so little, yet be told to embrace your rainy days
But I don't want rainy days,
I like sunshine and smiles to go along
with this happiness that I visit from time to time
So forgive me if I no longer get back to you,
because that is my definition of growth
I want deep laughter, slower conversations
and more peace in my life
Truth be told, I've
finally realized that not everyone
will make the cut in the changes
that I've made in my life

Grace

Silently…I want to open my heart
to God's grace and serve the purpose
that He has laid out for me
Prayerfully…I wish to sing the truth
in my heart, so there is no
contradiction in my daily actions
Hopefully…He can allow me to return
back to His favor, because I have
not taken heed to his great signs
Truthfully…I am done
trying to do things my way,
so I have chosen to surrender to His will
Regretfully…I must distance
myself from many whom I have
come to falsely depend on
Happily…I open my arms to a love
that I never thought would
ever come to wash me of my sins
Proudly…I shall now live
the way that our creator has already
made it out for me in this world
Humbly…I will accept His directions
and no longer stand in His way
of leading me through spirituality
Finally…without any reservations or expectations,
I give God full control over my spirit
as I attempt to be in His favor and grace…

A Perfect Lie

It has been a while since I've exposed a lie,
so let me try...
They say that we don't cry,
yet we have been known to flood
our hearts with self inflicted pains
In the eyes of the world,
we may seem perfect in familiarity
with divinity...but my sincerity is
my enemy when I paint this lie in me
Sometimes I live in my dreams,
too afraid to face these hard days
of heartbreaks, mind aches and fakes
who secretly crucify me,
when I speak with animosity, and act all godly...
most of you don't really know me,
but I hope you all hear me...
Blindly "they" say that I write perfectly,
yet I suffer nocturnally,
faithfully pray silently, and try to
smile constantly...even though
my weakness is never visibly to society...
But am I speaking of me, or vicariously
painting your struggles with clarity
even though you attempt to hide them constantly?
So as I scribble these words reluctantly...
would you say that I lie perfectly?

Choices

In these reflective times, I have
placed emphasis on the choices
that I have made in my life
The responsibilities of my decisions
have become my realities
The choices which have led me
to my present state of reflection
For I blame no one for my
circumstances and the position
that I usually find myself in
No one is to blame for the positives
nor the negatives that have shaped
my destiny and my daily paths
These lights around me, have dimmed
and brightened my life, due to the
roads that I have chosen to travel
But sometimes we tend to blame
society and other individuals
for our uncertainty,
even though inwardly, we know that
we are the navigators of our own choices...

On Your Road

On your road to success,
there will be stressful
days and lonely nights
Friends will leave and
family may even disappoint
Some will not see the struggle,
and only speak of your success
But that beautiful talent of yours,
was meant for the world to see
So fight the fear that keeps you
from getting out your dreams
And don't worry about those
who gossip and try to derail you...
they are just hidden fans who have
yet to see their own potential!

Individuality

You were meant for a glorious mission,
regardless of your present circumstances
Never succumb to the darkness
that comes to snatch away your
talents and passions or greatness
Remember what Moses accomplished,
what Samson used to slaughter the Philistines,
what David acquired for praising God,
what Job regained for being faithful,
what Abraham received for being obedient,
what Mary Magdalene gained for touching the divine garb,
what Joseph was blessed with for his hard work,
what life Lazarus received for his great belief,
what wisdom Solomon was embedded with for his great dedication,
what Gandhi attained with his new method,
what Mandela achieved with his unshaken faith in his people,
what Malcolm learned in his pilgrimage to Mecca,
what Obama achieved in the darkest hour...
And knowing all of this,
I still wonder why you still
fear your God given individuality...

Reality

The reality of things is that we fear
our true existence and the destiny that awaits us
We are too afraid to follow our own heart's
intentions, so we settle for what
our weak minds may have us do
We are too cowardly to seek out
our infinite possibilities, but instead descend
to the weakest positions which life may offer us
We are afraid to chance the thought that we are magnificent
beyond what others may label us
So we live our lives as reactive, rather than proactive
and our realities become what society expects
of us and we forever lead lives based on
empty promises along broken dreams
Lost dreams that cause frustration, stress
and the inability to see and/or accept a bright light
We become an embarrassment to our God given talents,
due to the struggles and misperceptions
of what life is really meant to offer
So I ask…what is your reality?

...Be careful...
that when you are being
praised for your great
work, that you are not
drunken with pride!
...Be humble...

Seeking
validation from
others only hinders
your personal growth
Measure your own
success by the love
you give, the hearts
that you heal, the souls
that you lead and the
completed work that
God put you on this
earth to do!

Religion

We now stand on the verge of our salvation!
In the halls of faith, many leaders
have used religion as a form of control
Some priests are forbidden to marry,
therefore fulfill their human desires
through the sadistic form of pedophilia
The masses hang on every word of some priests,
yet their leaders prey on their faith
in order to abstract money
and rob them of their diminished hope
Prayer and worship are highly emphasized
within many congregations...but
adultery, deceit and gossip dominate the "sheep"
Followers of the certain faith, seek
the redeemer, but the extremists have
tainted their image and caused the world to
stereotype the real intentions of their faithful followers
Glorification of war is constantly quoted through
ancient prophets and modern politicians,
but they all claim to be of peace and love
Religious practices have caused many to
defect and become atheists...
consciously subjecting themselves to
an unknown that awaits us all
The human race, as a whole, has lost its way,
strayed far from the true principles of religions,
regardless of faith, denomination, church or temple
The beauty of a Higher Power,
has been distorted and manipulated to satisfy
the selfish immoral desires of mankind
Souls have been misguided and spiritually broken
so they are unable to see the signs behind these human disasters
Condescendingly mocking the power of God
by placing their faith in deformed governments
Constantly judging others of separate
religions, bad mouthing one another...
instead of embracing the beauty of humanity
So let us ALL self-evaluate, self-check with humility

Broken

We have all been there…
Either we have been deceitful or fooled
We give our love selflessly and in return we are
undeniably broken by the mistrust
It matters not of race, gender or color…pain is unprejudiced
Fear of re-opening our hearts
turns us into pessimists when it comes to love,
so most give way to bitterness
Many remain dreamers rather than doers,
losing touch with reality and inevitably
resort to swimming in the oceans of despair
Faith becomes obsolete as stress
becomes our master in this type of war,
with no sight of peace for our distraught minds
Confusion leads many into making rash
decisions in choosing mates,
who distract them…instead of focusing them
towards the path of self-forgiveness
We struggle to persevere in the road of happiness,
unable to see the light beyond the pain
So when the so-called "one" arrives,
we are numb and quick to dismiss their kindness
with scornful assumptions…
because we are unable to differentiate
their love from our past aches
So we remain consistently angry, distant, lonely
and unable to acknowledge that we are merely broken…

Plan

You need a plan!
You need consistency,
so you can perfect whatever you are great at!
You need prayer, you need to believe
that you were meant to achieve
great things in your life!
Struggles are there
just to give you stronger character
You need to surround yourself with people
who will support you and
not downplay your focus and dedication
It's easy to have people around
who can always say yes...
but trust those who say no and
always give you constructive criticism
Don't forget to love and accept compliments,
regardless of how you've been treated
Be humble and confident,
so people feel at ease around you
Don't base your slow success
on what others have quickly achieved!
Know that where you are right now,
is where you are supposed to be
So don't question God's plan!

Extraordinary

To be exceptional,
you can not fear change
Be careful of the dream killers
who come as 'friends' and family...
Those who question your vision
are usually those closest to you
The hardest part is staying
consistent...so trust the
talent beating within
Remember that
God placed you on this
earth to do extraordinary
things...nothing less!

Lifetime

Sitting here….alone, silent, content,
thoughtful, repentant, yet hopeful
Much has come and gone,
as years of heartache and disappointments painted
a mural of what my life has become
They say that you must reach your lowest
in order to see the power of God,
but I beg to differ…
I have laughed to the point of tears,
loved with my every feeling
and experienced the beatings of life,
which hardly ever follow my heartbeats
So where do I stand?
I shut my eyes and openly embrace all
that is destined to consume me in this lifetime…

Restored

Humbly, I come before YOU
and ask YOU to cleanse me of all my sins
Make me whole and allow my flesh
to drink from the cup of righteousness
Bless the crown on my head with
immeasurable wisdom and my spirit
with everlasting humility
Give me serenity and forgive me for
the hearts that I have trespassed against
Guide my spirit to speak the truth
and teach me the obedience of a true disciple
Before YOU, I kneel and offer YOU my heart,
as did the great prophets
Even though my ways may at times
reflect the ignorance of a lost soul
Restore my faith as you did many others
and raise my spirit as you did those who obey
Make me as swift as the parables of life
and bless my eyes to see beyond this world's lies
Show me how to love as YOU loved
your only Begotten Son and allow my words
to shine as does the beauty of the sun…

Wives of Revolution

In silence…their tears are laid
out for prayers to heal
Nations weep for their departed leaders,
but the true cries remain soundless
Anguish overcomes the cause for
freedom and liberation
The tugging of the heart,
the sobbing of the soul,
the confirmation of the spirit,
is enough to leave any human in despair
Ntsiki *BIKO* sits quietly in a room,
wondering what is to become
of her life and her children
Her uncertainty is shared by
Pauline *LUMUMBA* and echoed by
Ana Maria *CABRAL*
Their hearts are filled with lingering
wails of disillusion and disbelief
Their trailing tears stream
toward the doorsteps of Aleida *GUEVARA*,
who also struggles to accept
the same daunting fate
that has stolen life's joy from the faces of
Betty *SHABAZZ* and Coretta *KING*…
endlessly attempting to soothe
the tears of Myrlie *EVERS,*
just before reaching out to
Laura Meneses Albizu *CAMPOS*
As children of liberation,
we must honor these powerful wives
and many other unsung heroic women
Wives of revolution who become
casualties of their husband's legacies
Solely stranded on this earth with
a famous last name…but fatherless children
Your tears, sorrows, pains,
prayers, hopes and struggles
will never go unheard
Your devotion is unmoved
Your strength is underrated
Your love is unquestioned
Our debt to *you*…unpaid!
-Dedicated to all wives of assassinated revolutionaries-

Bridge

Under our bridge,
we all have many pains and struggles
Struggles that have attempted
to steal our happiness
and push us into a state of doubt
Doubt can take away
the ability to rely on God's hope
Hope that we were never to
remain in a world that shuns
goodness and embraces darkness
Darkness that has no patience
for anyone who sees the light
of equality…above the spoils of society
Society that is accustomed
to playing with divinity,
as if it is not a reality
Reality allows us to face our fears
and bring truth to those
who remain faithless
Faithless is a dangerous thing to be
when we do not subscribe
to love, freedom, courage or peace…
as we stand over this bridge
of struggles and pains
that remains suspended over our lives…

Stop Searching

Everything you are searching
for...you already have!
You want love, yet you neglect
yourself. You seek success, but you don't
realize what you've already achieved.
You desire happiness, yet you don't
like your own beautiful smile.
You hope for change,
but everyday you're a different person.
You pray for blessings, but you're blessed to be awakened.
You look for peace, yet you battle yourself daily.
You expect everything, yet you do nothing to attain it.
Remember that love is internal,
success requires patience,
happiness is a process,
change is inevitable,
blessings are endless
and peace is necessary
to achieve anything!

Courage

Sometimes our faith is pushed
to test our inner strength
Our lives are changed by the
tribulations of unexpected events
Fear is not an option in the face
of trials and struggles
So day by day we cling on to the
beauty of hope and our future visions
The spirit may be tested,
but the soul is never broken
Sometimes we are unable to recognize
our own vigor and inspirations
Yet I see that the fight in you…it's everlasting
and your love is unshaken
Tears may flow joyfully and freely, as the images
of past memories overwhelm your heart
The epitome of your humanity,
your courage and your depth
are now on full display
No time for dismay or disheartening tears,
for God's grace is your daily bread
You breed inner beauty
as your *courage* exudes godliness
So I honor you,
pray for you,
barely know you,
but I infinitely admire you…

- In memory of Juana Luciano-

Imbalanced

Beyond the smiles, the false laughter,
the broken promises that lead
the bitterness away from love…
The endless struggles that add to
the tricky path to happiness…
The constant worries of financial instability…
The heartaches of daily trials
versus the ability to reach for joy…
The imbalance of society's demands
and the rebelling towards authority
The fear of aging,
and the mind hindering progress
because of past pains…
That is your imbalance!

Distant

I may seem distant...
Vulnerable to the cause
of my choices towards what
and whom I choose to love
I am never bitter,
even though my emotions
are distant from my reality
There is no pain, no tears,
just numb to my experiences
Maybe I am just focused
on my future and refuse to
be trapped by any pain
I am forever keeping my emotions
and my foolish ways far apart!

Change is Good

As time passes...things change!
Peace of mind becomes
more important
We want to learn more,
love a little stronger
Childish things are
finally put to rest
We appreciate simplicity,
worry less, smile often,
take our time,
learn to listen more intently
Fight less, make peace
with more people
Maturity sets in...
Life makes way
towards happiness,
as we seek a great inner
connection with
a higher power!

Interests

I am not interested in the
color of your skin
Nor in the religion that
you choose to practice
Your amount of money
does not impress me
I do not care for your
political affiliation
The country that you come
from is irrelevant to me
Your patriotism does
nothing for me
ALL I CARE IS:
How are you going to
love, care, change, mold,
benefit and better
our humanity?!

A Good Somebody

Sometimes being a good
somebody is what counts
Open the door for
a total stranger
Smile with someone
that touches your soul
Help the elderly
when they are struggling
Teach a child how
to respect and learn
Wipe away a tear with
kisses of joy
Fight for those who
are disabled or unable
A kind gesture can go a
long way...but being a good
somebody can change a heart!

Part of Life

It's ok to cry and reveal
your weaknesses
Eventually
we all breakdown and shed
those layers that kept us
imprisoned
Pain is a part
of life. Nevertheless...we
should all expect more
and as for those who hurt you...
well they are just lessons
to be remembered when
true happiness arrive

Touched

As I attempt to touch the dark
corner of this taboo subject...
let us inspect these scars of the soul
The repercussions of such an act
can leave life long wounds
Physically, mentally, emotionally...
the victim is no longer spiritually whole
Sitting alone...drowning in a river of tears,
unable to ever live freely
But the culprit is seldom an unknown being,
nor a faceless stranger
It is a smiling friend, a deceiving soul
that gains trust and easily manipulates
So the victim stares with empty eyes,
remains blinded by what they do not wish to see
Unable to comprehend the reasoning
behind their perpetrator's wicked act
Time may pass, yet the damage infiltrates the mind,
shatters the heart, and leaves sightless evidence
Gender is not a factor, race in non-existent,
but the hurt is evermore persistent
The spirit is violated beyond the realm of innocence,
as life veers off into a pathless wander
Ways of living go astray, blame is placed on the self,
as bitterness overwhelm the heart's ability
to ever trust or truly love again
Sadly...the pedophiles are protected,
political leaders are exonerated and compensated,
religious hierarchies are sheltered,
as families are desecrated,
and the victims are psychologically
ravaged from being touched...

-Dedicated to all sexually molested individuals-

Freedom

What if we were to walk the past path
that God created for us
and learn to shun the words of this dark world?
Would that bring about change in ourselves
and make us fight for peace?
But I sit here with no regrets
to any pain that was caused by anyone or anything
Singing hymns to the one
who has liberated me and the shackles
which had long rusted in my soul
Yet I wonder if it will last
or will it just be a temporary seclusion
from those who seek my downfall
At the end, I will still sing and give Him thanks,
due to the blessings that I have been given
So now I offer these blessings
of freedom to all of you
who seek to be free…

My Birthday

Today I celebrate another year...
Thankful to the Creator
for giving me endless blessings
I am humbly appreciative of everything
Most importantly the breath in my body
and the support of friends and family
Life can be beautiful and hard
at times...yet I'm grateful for its entirety
Nothing is ever a regret, as experience
has been my greatest teacher
So I happily think back and smile at
everything that I have achieved and
look forward to my future endeavors
Happiness, health, peace and love
are very important to me...
so I kneel and thank God for everything,
as I am humbled to have lived another year!

Letter To My Younger Self

If only I could go back in time and
speak to my younger self
First I would tell myself that my actions
need to be thought out more
Take your time, enjoy life a bit,
don't party too much and stay away from
some 'friends' because they will be toxic in the future
I would sit myself down, paint a picture
of a 'not so' bright future,
so my younger self could see that
hard work is very important in adulthood.
I would tell myself to not be so stubborn,
to listen more, talk less
Depend less on charm,
focus more on building intelligence
Be more aware of people's feelings, be more honest
I would teach myself to love slower,
smile more and dedicate myself
to being a better human being
But if YOU could go back in time...
what would YOU say to your younger self?

Old Age

The wonders of old age,
have always intrigued me
I have imagined
all that my age has to offer
I look forward to the simple sounds of
grandfatherhood and
the smiles of blissful grandchildren
running around freely
For I pray to see the days,
when I can embrace the elderly image
and reflect back on my life
But my path seems gloomy
and my struggles seem endless
Yet I rely on my faith to bring me
inner peace and old age,
even though it seems to be a lifetime away…

Discipline

We must condition our thoughts
to work towards the path
of infinite wisdom
Disciplining our hearts to beat
away from the sounds
of our minds
We must retain what
is the hardest to obtain…
We have to discipline our
spirits to seek only
the word and hand of God
Searching the soul for
the sounds which have led and
misled us through life
We must discipline the noises
that speak to us,
whenever no one hears us screaming
In those times we tend to find
ourselves by ourselves,
and with no one to give us peace
These are the times
of self-evaluation and self-discipline…

In My Loneliness

Inside the confusion of my mind,
you will find nothing
But loneliness is
a place where I retrieve to,
when the world becomes
too overwhelming
My loneliness is my haven,
my silence and my sanctuary
Here, you will find my deepest emotions
Here is where I hide my smiles
and bathe in joyful tears
Fears are unable to
touch my soul and pains
can't penetrate my spirit
Inside my loneliness, I disappear
from my daily struggles
Here, my struggles
never dictate my actions
And here, my heartbeats only move
to the rhythm of God's voice…

Reflect

Sometimes we allow our
accomplishments to overtake us
We lose focus of the gift that
we have been given
We tend to walk condescendingly
passed those who are going through
the same struggles that we have
personally overcome and struggled with before
So let us take a moment,
reflect on how far we've come
from the days of pain,
the stressful nights,
the dreaded tears...all of our past ways
Let us understand that helping others,
will indeed help us find our true selves
Let there be no difference between
you and those around you...
regardless of money, power or titles
Humble yourself and know that only
through humility will you ever
embrace your own humanity!

Faith

Faith is a hard concept for some…
We go through stages in our lives
and tend to foolishly question
the power of God and question
the struggles that we experience
But we are a strong humanity,
full of faith and we have the ability
to overcome, as we believe
He has put us here to succeed...
but with some struggle
our spirits will only be empowered
Faith is the understanding
that you will get through anything,
succeed with a smile,
then help others to learn how to overcome
Nothing lasts forever and
everything has its season
So remain steadfast,
pray with conviction and know that
faith is nothing without works.

Pride

Pride has long kept me from getting
to where I'd like to be in my life
Sometimes I blamed others for my struggles
and even held back my feelings
when love came calling
My pride became emotionally
damaging and it pushed my 'calling' further away
But I have freed myself,
learned to take my time with love,
worked with more passion,
even wrote with happiness,
and always spoke with conviction
Don't allow pride or anything else
hold you back from reaching your dreams
Pride is what keeps
most people from trying and fearful
of failing! So learn from your mistakes,
find your talent and do what God put
you on this beautiful earth to do!

Learn To Forgive

One of the hardest things to do in life is forgive…
Being wronged, leaves us angry, bitter,
questioning ourselves and in a state of confusion
The pain can be overwhelming,
the strength to overcome may be too small
So we remain in a dark corner,
seeing that reflective light of
forgiveness in the background
But in order to walk in personal acceptance,
life long happiness and freedom,
we must learn to forgive
Bitterness holds too much power,
anger breaks us down daily,
and confusion requires too much attention...so let go
Cry it out, laugh at your past,
know that it happened for a reason
I know that it is easier said than done...
but it is the only way to ever receive what you were
meant to have in your lifetime
Forgiveness is a powerful tool,
it is not for the those who have wronged you,
hurt you, slandered you...
it is for your own peace of mind!

Who Are You?

You are beautiful beyond imagination.
You smile, laugh, hurt, cry,
and love just as the rest of us on earth
There is no difference between the lives
of others and the breath that is within you
So don't ever let anyone tell you that you are weaker,
superior or inferior than any other being
Your heart is as sacred as the others who walk this land
You are diverse for a reason, because you were
created to stand out...as we all were
But that is the beauty of diversity
and the different shades of skin tone,
the shapes of curves, the lengths of hair...
the style of clothes.
What you have done,
has already been created under the sun,
therefore do it better
So shine when the spotlight is on you,
because your diversity is what sparks
the minds of those who don't look like you,
walk like you, speak like you...so be you
You are a gift!

Time

In these dark times in life,
I think back to the true revelations of my life
Times of peace and obedience,
instead of times of ignorance and violence
At times I dream of the past
and hear the voices of great prophets
But at the same time, I ask myself,
is it just a hallucination of mine?
So I now own the freedom to think,
therefore I stand in silence for those of the past
who have made this time possible
But time waits for no man,
So they say…
If that is true, then why have most been
infected with the plague of time,
since the beginning of time?
Time is a strange thing to those who barely sleep
So are we all to reap
what the world's leaders sow?
And if so, will my time spent on earth
count only in the echoes of eternity?
Time is meaningless to those
who dare to dream, or should I say,
those who chase a life-long dream
For many say that time is everything…
But I wonder what will they say,
when I tell them that I timed my dream perfectly
And when I reached that ever-so powerful dream of mine,
I found it to be just a dream
A dream that had distracted my visions,
And taken all of my life's time!

Religion (Part 2)

It is sad what our world has succumb to!
We are quick to dismiss and close our minds
to what does not agree with our own beliefs
Sadly it's the religious types that are
usually more judgmental, hypocritical
and analytical than others
Scriptures are used to blind the people,
turning them into visionless sheep,
who are fearful of questioning their
pastor/father/preacher/guru/imam!
Religion is supposed to spread love and
offer peace to those who struggle...
instead it is used as a justification for war,
a cash cow, a fear factor and the greatest weapon
used in the separation of race, gender and color!
It is time to question these men/women
who have chosen religion to mentally enslave
those who fear what may come in the afterlife!

Time Again

I wish for nothing more than
to have time again on my hands
Time to look beyond my emotions
and beyond my pains
I have nothing left
but the images of my past
A past which consumed me
and removed love out of my life
See, my time was never precious
and my time was
always beyond any other's lifetime
I was caught between the future that awaited me
and the presence
that had always overwhelmed me
All I had was the past,
which haunted me and unabled me to move on
So my time was irrelevant
to my happiness, because I felt that God's
peace had long deserted me
Thus, I was left between
the sounds of my life, the minutes of
an hour and the hours of each day
So time meant nothing to my thoughts,
or to anything beating within me
Therefore I remained without the
perfect timing of anyone that had ever loved me…

Betray

We are indeed blinded by ambitions
which betray our very needs
Seeking out to embrace the lies
of this weak and lost world
We sing spiritual hymns in the silent halls
of our heart's loneliness
In exchange, we receive simple loves
and heartbreaking agonies
At the end, we are left with insecurities
and endless questions of trust
Questions which in then leads us to live
our lives in fear of internal pain
A pain which is brought forth
by the innocence of our protected hearts
Yet it betrays us and allow us
to become vulnerable in the hands
of those who never appreciate
the strengths of our love…

Take Your Time

Time is the most precious thing
in this world. We are so busy with
our schedules that we forget to
enjoy our lives. When old folks tell us to take our time,
we usually just brush it off.
Not realizing that all we do is live
in the memory of great times.
So be grateful for every breath,
smile a bit more, love a little slower,
walk in peace a bit further.
Enjoy your family, honor those who raised you,
live with a passionate heart,
dance with no worries and always speak
with absolute conviction! Don't waste time
worrying about the past, nor the future,
live every minute as if your last day was revealed
to you at birth. Time...it passes by so
swiftly and most of us never come close
to enjoying the beauties of our lives.
So take your time!

Just Feel It

In life you will feel what is real, and
what is fake...will eventually unravel
There is no such thing as a
gut feeling, it's God tapping into
your intuition and giving you warnings
Worrying is a waste of time,
scars are testaments of your strength,
love is a journey of pain & joy,
wars are reminders of mankind's greed,
patience is a virtue of faith
So never mind what 'they' say about
you, focus on where you're headed
Complaining only postpones progress,
because 'they' are not the problem
for your personal lack of progression in life
YOU are the one holding up your own dreams,
happiness, love and success!

Believe

Everything happens for a reason...
remember that you can't control destiny
The struggles become harder,
when you feel you can't take it anymore
Just because things fall apart,
it doesn't mean that you have to fall apart
Some relationships just aren't meant to be
and 'good' things are taken away,
in order to make space for 'greater' things to come
I know life is hard, but we are all built for trying times
So don't drown in your tears,
don't allow stress to take you under...
scream out your pains and the frustration in your heart,
so you can be renewed. You were meant for greatness,
but you must go through some things first
in order to achieve it
Happiness, love and peace only come
to those who have faith and patience...
no need to rush,
take your time walking to your destiny!

EMPIRE

Arrogance is the antithesis of humility!
So let us latch on to acceptance of our fellow beings
and shun the notion of separation
For we are destinies to our own light...as we shall never
compromise with the enticement of darkness
Let us all stare at our own distorted images of
judgments in the mirror of self-evaluation
Analyzing our own inhumanities,
before pointing out the insecurities of others
Some may belittle others with speeches of civilization,
yet they themselves act far from civilized
Criticism is just an excuse to develop
one's own vanity...when lost in their own false spirituality
So build pride in humanity...internationally,
and not just a hopeless love nationally
Pray for blessings of nations, rather than isolation
When asking for forgiveness, make sure to always
offer the forgiver...hope, peace and love
Seek to turn adversaries into allies,
as unpopular opinion will forever be
the enemy of your conscience
Shun secret societies, immoral religious institutions,
corrupt government agencies and all power seekers
Know that the power of good...far outweighs
the temptation of harmful and evil deeds
Beware of your own lust for drunken dominance...
For empires are forged by empty men, who
shun the idea of knowing their own weakness(es)
Thus forever ostracizing a greater love for mankind...
as they are dictated to by their own malign mental empire
End it or it will end you!

Live

Life is short, it really is...
so wasting time because of fear
or protective of any other's emotions,
is a disservice to one's own heart
I want to bathe my heart in truth,
so I refuse to try to force anything...
I'm just going to let life come freely!
Just speaking what I feel...
we waste so much time, months, years...
being so dishonest with ourselves and
fighting back our own feelings
I will never do that again!
I owe it to my happiness,
to give it a chance and not
try to control everything!

Perseverance

We've all had a time in our lives
that we were tested
We lose focus, question hope, seek an escape...
to no avail. Everyone has been in this position,
at least once. Friends can't help,
family is powerless to get you out of it.
It is your war to fight, it is your
battle to win or succumb to. But you were
created in the image of a powerful God,
so the victory is within you.
So seek and you shall find that fighter
in you to surpass anything that drops you,
weakens you, makes you feel worthless.
Rise and understand that you are stronger than you know,
feel that fervor of overcoming...
and when you smile and you feel rejuvenated,
you will know that you will always
have the spirit of perseverance!

Broken People

There are broken people everywhere!
Daughters who are seeking
love and acceptance from their fathers
Sons helplessly watching their mothers
struggle to make ends meet
Inmates silently crying in their cells,
governments toppled by their citizens,
presidents creating wars on the back
of innocents, lives being taken
without any regards for a conscience
We are living in scary times,
stressful nights and fearful days
Love, patience, compassion and
empathy have been traded in for
hate, greed, murder and vanity
We live in a broken world...so
I pray for God's everlasting
forgiveness and mercy for us all

In the Moment

It is the moment when you realize that
your dreams have the ability to awaken the world
The endless nights when you struggle
and stop yourself from quitting on your talents
because you see what lies ahead
When your heart and mind
battle for supremacy over your spirit
It is the moment when life becomes
too hard to bear,
so your tears help you persevere
When fears grip you and try to keep you
from pushing through the pain, struggle and anguish
At times the vision may become blurry and
the fog of doubts become blinding,
as you feel misunderstood
But these are the moments that are captured
within seconds and rest on lifelong decisions
It is when the love in your eyes drip through your hopes
and slowly linger with your words
These moments are timeless,
they are secured within us forever,
and encapsulated evermore in our dear hearts
So live free,
smile more often,
love with no expectations,
work with no worries,
dance with no fear,
play with no restrictions,
give without any reservations,
forgive with no bitterness,
listen with patience,
speak with kindness...
and know that life is about living in the moment!

Secrets

I hold the untold secrets and
pains that have long kept me captive
This heart of mine is weak and
broken by my own divulged expectations
I want to learn to love
in another language…so I can be renewed
Move to a spiritual inner place where
peace brings me to a time with no end
and oceans of happiness become my daily bread
Maybe I am just dreaming
and falsely wishing for a hope
that has long been deported from these shores
So in the meantime…I will continue with
my half smiles,
my limping heart,
my hollow words,
my vanishing desires,
my façade of strengths
and my faithful aspirations…
as I continue to dwell in the safety
of my own secrets!

Small Light

Inside we all hold a special light…
Our own *small light* that is displayed through our
ability to make others smile and feel good
We are all given a special gift
to perfect and then manifest it unto the world
This talent is embedded in us all
for the betterment of all mankind
So chase your dreams vehemently,
be who you have always aspired to be
Never allow the opinion of anyone
to deter you from your path of greatness
Forever surround yourself with
those who urge you to perform at a higher level
Always know that prominence is measured
by those that you endlessly help,
yet never forget that you will forever
be riddled with criticism
So let that small light of yours shine,
let your work brighten up the lives of those
close to you and those who remain unknown
Never shy from your Godly blessing,
because you were meant to inspire all people
Remember that your journey
was created to bring joy
and cause a ripple of happiness
to overflow in making a way
for the spreading of worldly love
Let it be known
that you were made to excel,
molded to lead humbly,
appointed to innovate
and exalted to bring forth
everyone's small light!

Journey

Even though the world may call,
it does not mean that you
have to always respond
Sometimes silence is needed
for things to become clear
When life becomes hard,
it is alright to disappear,
in order to regain peace of mind
Maybe it is time for me to
evaluate my choices and see why I
stand where I am now in life
I have learned that becoming numb
to my reality…can at times
be a gift and a curse
Constantly confusing my own clarity
because these tears refuse to come
down and cleanse my pain
No one knows what I
go through on a daily basis
So I tend to stay away
because my heart is too tender
At the end….
we are all addicts to something,
but I just hope that we can convert
our addictions to great passions,
and free ourselves,
before finding our "calling"
in this great journey…

Addiction

Addiction is a powerful entity!
Anything can be addictive,
it can become a chain on your spirit,
making you a slave to its power
You shy away from life's light,
basking in the misery of darkness
It can drag you to the pits of despair...
leaving you broken,
feeling unworthy and subhuman
But you can rise,
fight for your freedom,
no longer accepting the
pain that it has brought you
Slowly walking away from that shackle...
which has kept you from your happiness
So declare that you will run away from your addiction,
never going back to that mindset
that has been controlled by that drug,
that alcohol, that false love
Break free, know your worth,
bathe your temple in the halls
of freedom. Then reach back
and help anyone who has been
controlled by an addiction!

Everything is easier said…
But how can I gain the
strength to get it done?
We are creatures of habit,
so we continually do what
we seek NOT to do
We endlessly say to ourselves:
One day I am going to
workout and get healthy
For my children's sake
I am going to put down
that drink and
get my life together
Soon I will embrace
my spirituality and
get closer to God
Tomorrow I am going
to stop smoking,
so I can live to see my
grandchildren age gracefully
Maybe I should start
saving more on needs
and spend less on wants
I hope to soon get the courage to reveal
my true love with no fear
Shortly I expect to reach
my goals and stop questioning
my God given talents
Next year I will return back
to school and get that degree
We all have things in life
that we want to get done,
yet we always put them off
for a convenient time
I understand that things are hard,
but never impossible
Yet we rely on excuses
and rest on the notion that
"they" will eventually get done
Even though we all know
that "they" are just easier said…than done!

Humans

Those of weak hearts will
forever fear change
They will part from the
union of equality and
always create chaos
As they speak of peace in
daylight, war is created
when night falls
Politics and propaganda
will remain vital tools
in the creation of empires
Separation will come from religion,
social class and financial status
But be of a good heart,
flee from wrongdoing,
and keep your heart filled
with love…as you
continue to help the poor!

Speak Your Mind

Never hold on to your words…
regret is your worst enemy!
Remember that our time
here is very limited
Do not be afraid of failing
because you were created
in the image of success
Run towards your dreams
and bring others with you,
it is never too late…
Speak your heart and always
follow your passions
Fear and love can not occupy
the same space…
so do not doubt yourself
Work in faith, play in joy,
pray in silence,
smile in happiness,
rise in confidence!

Prayer

I pray to have the ways of Jacob,
yet it still pains me to
see the struggles
of my brother and all others
The words of Solomon
have given me much wisdom,
but discipline has yet to
display my ways
My days are long
and troublesome,
as were those of Job,
even though my patience
is but a muster seed of His
This world has given
me the struggles of David,
as God continues to bless
me with the persistence of Moses.

Humanity

Perception can be deceiving…
Many complain about
the material trappings that
they do not possess
Forgetting about the tsunami
stricken, the war ravaged,
the poor and the hungry
Disregarding humanity,
ignoring blessings,
and shunning simplicity
Life has become about perception…
how it is seen, fixed, molded,
lived or left behind
These things create the basis
behind one's personal
"half empty/half full" factor
So take your time and
be thankful for everything
that you come to experience!

Lasting Impression

When it's your time to go...you must
leave a lasting impression for all
You must be of great stature,
full of truths and love...but also intrigue
You must be passionate about
your beliefs, execute them with
authority and absolute conviction
You must not bend to the will
of anything or anyone that
throws you off your path
There is no time to question your
destiny or your lasting legacy
If you want to be remembered,
then transcend the unexpected,
be unpredictable and never allow
the world to know you entirely
Many may claim to love and
support you, but some can be
deceived by their own ambition
So be careful of whom you share
your ideas and plans with...
especially those whose sole ambition is to bask
in the success of your dreams!

-LOVE-

Love

The simplicity of this word is rather at times
too complex for the human mind.
Love is pure and untainted, and it has various levels to it.
Love is unattached and free of all holds.
It can not be sought after, for it can
only be attained through patience.
There is no such thing as a "painful" love.
Love does not have the ability to cause pain,
but the illusion of love can cause pain.
Pain comes from expectation, as one may say to another:
"I expect you to love me as I love you"
This expectation in time causes disappointment,
which brings forth pain.
Hence, love does not cause pain!
Love is like the wind, it is powerful and
consuming, yet one can not see it.
There is no envy, nor jealousy in being loved
or having love for one another being.
Love has no flaw and it is unquestioned.
Worshipping anything or anyone,
either it being religious or secular is not love.
Worshipping something or someone derives from fear,
and fear & love can not occupy the same space.
One can not love his or her mate and fear them at equal time.
Can one love and worship his/her God?
I believe so, because God is created in our image;
thus we worship ourselves when we
say we love and worship God.
One expects God to rescue one from his/her struggles,
therefore the question of love and
expectation comes into mind.
But love has the ability to liberate a rusty soul
and a weary body.
Love allows freedom to flow throughout
the world and in every household.
Love is a man treating his woman
like a Queen and not a princess.
Love is a woman referring to her man as a King,
rather than just a prince.
Love is living and allowing others to live
in a world that is free of hate,
jealousy, expectations and envy!
So what is love to you?

Purpose of Love

Love…such a powerful and sweet word
But we, as humans,
have desecrated its importance
and have imposed our own
definition of what it is meant to be
Love is silent and sightless
It is beyond the outstretched hands of time
and its significance is beyond our own understandings
Love is when one reveals the tears of joy,
it is when the soul and spirit align themselves
along the sweet whispers of God
It is unconditional and it only requires
total submission, in order for it to manifest itself
The purpose of love is as simple as
a child smiling at his/her parent
It is the purpose of protection from the world,
for love is an endless path
Love is when you look at your partner
and you see nothing but truth,
honesty, patience & humility
My purpose of love is to liberate
the shackles of pain….
and bring sweet elation,
and smiles to all faces that have struggled
with life's daily hardships
But what is your purpose of love?

This or That?

Sometimes I wonder, I just wonder...
So you let me know: will it be this or that???
With this: he will treat you like a queen,
love you until you brag to your friends about how great he is
But with that: he may slap you, embarrass you,
and only sex you in order to keep you
With this: she will wash your clothes,
cook your food and rub your back
But with that: she may flirt with your friends,
cuss you out, and max out your credit cards...
yet you will still be attracted to how "fine" she is
With this: he may pay off your debt, make you dinner,
send you to a spa when you seem overworked
But with that: he will stay out all night, steal your happiness,
call you out your name and verbally abuse you
With this: she will take you to God with her,
surprise you with lunch and help you reach your goals
But with that: she will always party,
refuse to do laundry, and only cook
when your "successful" friends are coming over
With this: he will respect your parents,
speak of marriage and surprise you with flowers
But with that: he will say that he loves you,
but is not "in" love with you, forget your birthday,
and becomes intimidated by your success
With this: she will always be faithful,
take care of you when you're sick,
and voluntarily pick you up
when your car breaks down
But with that: when you lose your job,
she's on to the next man,
always want to attend the latest parties
and bad mouth you for giving her a "small" ring
With this: he will tell you that you're a blessing from God,
always think of you before himself
and tell his mother that you're definitely the one
But with that: he will constantly ignore your phone calls,
his lies are never ending and he says
that marriage & kids...just don't fall into his life plan
WITH THIS: *love* is first-WITH THAT: sex is first
So what will it be: this or that?

Unseen

I just want to hold your hand,
learn where you wish to take your life's desires
and place my thoughts alongside your ambitions
I do not want to romance you nor buy you jewelry,
I just want to see and learn
how you truly wish to be loved
I want you to yearn for my conversation,
my silent walks in faith,
and the simple things
that life has brought me
In return, I want to build with you,
see God's love in your eyes,
as we share a first date in peace
I do not want to be your lover,
nor your entertainment,
I just want to be your partner,
who relieves the world's pains from your mind
and eases the beatings of your heart,
while consistently showing you the path
of what love really entails
But how can we enjoy every second,
hour, day, year, decade, and God willing, a century,
if I still remain unheard
and your true intentions remain unseen?

Sanctuary

In you…
in you I find peace!
Peace of mind and pieces of God's sanctuary
You are my Sheba and I am your Solomon
Thus…you have come to pass
Silently passing through my spirit,
before grazing my soul with your grace
Your words are mere temples of silence,
yet your smiles leave me speechless
But who are you and what place
have you taken my dreams to?
I dreamed in dimensional sectors
and multiplied your heart's decimals
into different divisions,
before you had the chance to subtract
my thoughts from adding you to my mission,
even though I was never a mathematician…
I reach for your light continually
and pray throughout our conversations,
for our God's revelations
Thus, you are infinite
So I travel through your visions
and gain blessings for inquiring
all of your inquisitions
Perhaps if I train my spirit
to walk before me, then my soul
can reach you before you forsake me
But who am I to question your destiny?
The destiny that has long depleted my missions
throughout the shores of your oceans
For you are now in proximity,
therefore I must now decipher your sanctuary…

Serenade

They want to serenade me with
applause and compliments
They want to honor me, put me
on stages and tell the world
how great my words are
They want to give me sweet gifts,
bathe me in the luxuries of life,
spoil me for sharing my 'talent'
They want to love me, for constantly
showing them how to really love
themselves through my work
They want to celebrate my accomplishments
and offer me everything that this
beautiful earth has to offer
But in the mean time, I just want
to look from atop that stage
and see your smile
So you know that YOU are
the reason that I reached
my greatest level!

Alone with You

Whenever I am near you,
I feel like I'm baptized in an
ocean of endless bliss
Your scent beholds me,
your kind heart is a thing of beauty,
your mind keeps me engaged,
you are all that I ask for
With every blink,
I take pictures of you,
so when we part,
I close my eyes and
replay you in my mind
Whenever I'm alone with
you, the world stands still,
my heartbeats get louder,
true love is revealed
I want to feel this feeling
until the next time that
I am alone with you...

Penetrate

Dented slightly into
your anatomy
Confined into your entity
that tends to control me
It's beyond this life,
surpassing visual eroticism
It binds us, closely knit
and perfectly sewed together
Coming apart will be hard,
as we mingle in slants
Silence is the loudest noise
as I make you my muse and use
your breathing for inspiration
Beyond these earthly walls,
we transport to the next life...deep
into each other's psyche,
no excuses...penetrating the mind!

Crossed

In the wind's grace
your sounds revealed my words
For you were the rainy
drops in my soul
So I became your soil,
rich in grain
and rich in urban herbs
But you filled my spirit
with your love in vain
I thought you were
the image of the biblical Sarah,
and I had been promised
the covenant of Abraham
But you no longer
yearned for me to recite you
my poetic vibes
So at the crossroads,
your heart crossed me infinitely
For you are the reason why
my soul and spirit have
engaged in a spiritual civil war...

Real Love

I will not settle for security…
Security of a false relationship,
out of fear of ending up alone
I do not just want to love,
I want to be fully "in" love
I refuse to be with someone
just because my friends or family
get along with that person…
and at the end, I remain in misery
I want to be able to have a
connection with my mate
Mentally, spiritually & physically,
I want to fully allow them in
Some say that love is God given,
so I am going to wait on that beautiful gift
I want my partner to be my
best friend, my greatest challenge,
my admirer, my critic,
but also my greatest supporter
I want to feel as if I can not
live without their words or their touch
When people say that they are
waiting for the real thing,
they are actually saying that they
want to love and be loved mutually…
I now understand this is the
real love that we all pray for…

Bitter End

Sometimes love is not enough!
Enough to hold me
in the dreams that
we created together
The hurt, the pain,
the tears of fighting for
a relationship that was
only based on hope
We both swam in different
strides...so we were oceans apart
How could I have denied you,
I could not imagine this
world without you,
loving you selfishly,
because I wouldn't want
any other hands touching you
You were what I deserved,
so I no longer settled
for cheap settlements,
We were similar to no other,
So you imprisoned me, shackled me
because I only wanted to be
placed in your confinement
You deserved the happiness
that I held for you,
no matter what struggles & pains
it took to arrive at this destination…
knowingly that I was
your final destination
But we remained distant in our
hearts & minds...unable
to align our happiness with
our hopes of a future
For we suffered in distant pieces,
shattered by love,
unable to trust or
give ourselves to what
we deserved...thus forever remaining
in the bitter end of misery!

Pretty Insecurity

Wanting me to stay,
but I continue to view your intentions
as defense mechanisms,
using my love as relief for your scars...
even though I have nothing
to do with your past.
I fight to please you in the present
because I see us in a brighter future
For He said that I would be
a blessed man in finding a wife,
a similar reflection of me...
but I'm constantly distracted
by those who follow me,
instead of you standing beside me...
So I plead for your forgiveness,
I sought to blame you for our separation,
but in reality, it was the contradiction within me
that made you move away from me
and into the city of heartbreak!
Beauty can not describe the Heavens in your smile,
so I steal a glimpse of you,
while you sit amongst others,
as the horns in my own mind
blare louder that you can foresee...
Singing me sweet songs of peace,
but your chaotic heart and unstable mind
puts you in a state of confliction...
How can I love you, yet fearing that your love
beats for someone, somewhere else with a pretty insecurity...
We are close as the ocean and sand,
yet our shores barely touch the surface of our possibilities...
but infinitely we will continue with the inability
to show our true selves to one another...

Reciprocity

I would be lying if I said that I love
you and didn't expect it in return
Friend or mate...I give you
my all and hope that in time of need,
you will always reach out to me
I want your support,
your criticism and for you
to push me in the right direction
whenever I tend to lose focus
I want you to make me smile,
help me reach my goals,
and when things aren't alright,
you'll always be there for me
But if you don't or can't...it's ok,
because whatever purpose
you were meant to play in my
life...I thank you in advance!

Possibly

I want to possibly…
give you reasons to smile
Tear down your walls
Keep you mentally
& spiritually focused on HIM
Make you the envy of all
Show you how insecurities
are just a state of mind
Pray that you are forever my grace
Show you how jealousy is
more cancerous than lust
Take my time with you,
so when you breathe,
you instantly inhale my love
Show you that your spirit has already
connected with my soul
Touch me slow,
love me whether I am high or low,
as I sit here and hope that you will
give us a chance to grow...

Vulnerability

Imagine you were beside me,
painting a reality
that was relatively
free of any insecurity,
but overflowing with
your love's complexity,
so it is hard to be me,
when there is no we
Must I pay society or a love's fee
in order to have thee
or kiss you where your neck be?
This instability is killing me,
so hopefully I can slowly
have you smiling happily
at this love in me
which made you blush
surprisingly and shyly...
I tried to come off
confidently, but at the end
I only breathed you in me
quietly, because I was too
afraid of my own vulnerability...

Pledge my Allegiance

I pledge allegiance
to your heart
Being a part of your
simple desires,
lighting & putting out
all of your fires
Raise you high,
so they all stare at your beauty
Write you love letters,
hide our pictures in various
places, so you can randomly find them...
just to see you smile
Kiss your fingertips,
massage your mind
after a long day away
Relieve your stress,
take my time when I caress
Make you feel blessed,
while the rest wonder
why you adore me carelessly,
but in reality,
they are full of envy
Stop.....now kiss me!

Too Good To Be True

Even though they say that I write you books
with the most elaborate words,
you have yet to know how much I adore you
You have fulfilled all that I
had hoped to find in a mate
This blessing of God's creation
has enveloped me and protected me
through the stormiest days
You have found ways to infiltrate my heart,
that I had always
claimed to be confidential
At times, I smile and say that you are
too good to be true,
because I have never felt the way
that you make me feel
For you, I will silence the world and
live within the beatings
of your blissful heart
Just seeing your face,
brings forth unending pleasure and joy
to my soul and spirit
For you are the epitome of poetry
and the reasoning behind God
creating a companion for me
See, you are a reflection of eternity…
Hence, you are too good to
be true for me…

The End

As it may seem to the world
and to those who know us not,
the flame from our hearts has disappeared
The anticipation of seeing your smile
and caressing your face has long gone
The songs that I sung to you in my dreams
have begun to skip,
because you have scratched
my love from your eyes
The fire which once displayed our feelings,
now only burn in the flame
of our endless arguments
The lies, the hypocrisies and the false
hopes in your words
have long drenched my mind
and the peace in my heart
Sadly I now only love you,
without being in love with you
Therefore I can no longer lie to myself
and allow you to sing me
false hopes of a bright future

Possibility

There may be a possibility
of she being a worthy adversary
One who questions me of my intentions
without any resignation
For she is patient and humble,
yet I wonder of her motives
This beautiful being has kept my mind
in its natural and undisturbed state
Even though I have renounced
the ignoble notion of love
She has sparked my interest and caused
me to reevaluate my thoughts
But will I lose my sanity,
as I search for the simplicity of
her heart's reality?
This is a difficulty
that has merely created a sigh
of possibility within me
A possibility that is unfailingly,
yet at the same time with uncertainty
Nevertheless it is a possibility
which has long evaded me..

Blinded Love

Many say that it will eventually
come to an end and shatter
The love that I believed
would never come to be,
has embodied me and my identity
At times, fear grips my soul
due to the questions of my heart
Inquisitions of eternal connections
between this being and I
Even though we have yet to state
our infinite vows to the world
For my shattered past has led me
to question the motions of your love
But I have yet to find any faults
in your eyes or any lies in your words
You soothe all of my pains and
keep me sane in the midst of all these rains
But will your reign of love eventually
come to a painful end
and shatter all that I have been a part of?
Only time shall reveal
what this blinded love has concealed…

Bitter Misery

I had given it all up,
just to taste the sweetness of your love
The love that seduced my heart
and painted illusions in my mind
I once believed that you
were one of a kind
But my intuition betrayed my conscience
and allowed you into my spirit
Therefore my love no longer had a limit
or a common destination
As you were given total access to the
secret codes of my personal world
And in time, you penetrated my inhibitions
and gave my life new visions
But time took its toll on our vows
and pains began to set in
The end was inevitable,
but I held on to the sweet misery of your love
Time passed as you began
to elude my words and only
sought after my touch
But it did not take much for me
to complete my paces to infinity
Even though I was saddened
by your tears, I could no longer
dwell in the bitterness of our misery…

Revolutionary Love

We were meant to breathe the same air and
fight the revolution together
Maybe if we were to live in the ocean,
then maybe we could be silent
and only speak with our eyes
We can offer our fears to one another
and gain our blessings
by just professing our devotion to the world
and seeking our revolutionary love
But then our destinies would lie in the
hands of others, who only seek to pillage
the dreams that we have shared and
promised to one another
Everyday I walk backwards in search
of my female soldier who fought her
way out of my heart and infinitely
into my mind…

Blinded

Somehow, someway I am consumed
by the essence of this beautiful being
At times, I find myself gathering
your departed scent and
bathing in your lingering presence
For it overwhelms me
and causes me to conform to your image
Blind to the fact of your true intentions
and your false and feeble confessions
Confessions with bits of truth and the endless
plots of lies that I despise
But I am caught within the beauty
of your eyes and what you epitomize
See, I know that I have been blinded
by the power of your love
and your false oath
Yet I am unable to remove your smiles
from the corners of my mind,
thus I shall forever remain blinded…

Anticipation

Have you ever waited
anxiously by the phone?
Stared at someone with a
calm in your spirit and a
peace in your soul?
Connected spiritually
as well as mentally?
But afraid to say the wrong
thing and mess up everything?
Smiled whenever their voice
and touch came to mind?
Did your heart race when
you were going to meet up?
Became overly shy when you
were complimented?
Felt overly excited when the
future seemed possible with that special one?
You mean everything to the world,
but that one person means the world to you
What a feeling this is...

Don't Hold Back

If you're going to love me,
make it real...
I need the kind of love that
causes me to think of you and desire
to always be near your side
The love which has that once in a lifetime,
passionate, powerful and unexplainable type of feeling
If we're going to fall in love,
then let it be known that fights are inevitable
But the happiness that I offer...
is beyond anything you'll ever experience
I'm going to need you to trust me
and give me your entire heart,
without holding back anything...kind of love
Don't assume nor create thoughts
that connect me to any of your past pains
or my past mistakes as well
Encourage me and help me reach these goals
so we can enjoy the rewards
If you're going to love me,
don't hold back to see how much I love you,
just love me and make me feel alive!

You

I breathed you, inhaled you, but
refused to succumb to the
thought of ever exhaling you
You've taken my mind to a
new form of freedom
Got me prancing in ecstasy,
inevitably you became my truest reality
There is no other entity that takes me,
swivels me, feeds me, plunges me...
This dance is instrumentally made
for the world to see and possibly envy
Similar to a deity, inhuman,
got me wooing because your
words are shattering me,
replacing the old me, then rebuilding, creating,
assimilating to a new pattern of rapture
This is no longer just enticing,
but overriding my old ways,
redirecting what I have learned
in all of my ages, so flow with me freely
because my book has reopened,
as your penmanship is etched
clearly in phases
of my newly blank pages!
You are my poetry!

Thief in the Night

You stole my love from
the confinement
of my hidden heart
I fought the urge,
told myself that you
weren't worth it
Ignored your smiles,
ran away from your touch
But I was no match
for your persistence
For God had already
aligned you with my spirit
So my soul gave in
and bathed in your ocean
My sands became
addicted to your shores
You kept me at bay!

Expectations

...it was not attention
that she desired
Nor sweet words
to be expected
She had her
own security
So from me,
she only
required love
But I was broken,
and trying to
find myself
So I left,
empty, full of
fear and with
no place to go...
but just far away
from her
expectations

Encouragement

Everyday I rise and put effort in changing
the circumstances of my life
As my friend and fellow human being
in this journey, I just need you
to encourage me
Sometimes I get down and break down...
yet I never see myself giving up
Your words give me light,
you breathe life into my struggle
and it always remind me that
I am here to encourage others
I always look forward to your honesty
and your criticism...
you make me a better person
I don't have time for games, lies or useless pity...
so regardless of wherever we stand,
just know I thank YOU for
always being in my life,
loving me without judgment and being truthful!

Captivated

Seldom am I speechless
in the presence of such a rarity
My eyes widened at the image of such
a beautiful being
It was at this point in my life
that I was consumed by a fear
that would never allow me
to encompass your heart
So I just remained content
with our simple conversations
Offered you my inner peace
in exchange for your outer wars
And at the end,
we were both captivated
by the irregularity
of each other's simplicity…

Anniversary

Everyday I have come to celebrate you,
on every hour, after every laughter,
during every kiss and every embrace
You are my anniversary of life…
The reasoning behind the connection
of two souls becoming one
No ring, no ceremony, no wedding
can ever define what my spirit owes your soul
For your smile, I will gladly
make a fool of myself amongst all
The hopes of a marriage stand
on the shoulders of God's love
So I pray daily for our union
cry before our maker, because
I have been fortunate to be in your space
For this, I make you my daily anniversary,
my celebration of life
with our beautiful children
You are my everything, my pride,
my evolution, my daily anticipation
I want to be your loyalty,
the one you seek in misery and joy,
so we can pray together and strengthen
one another…in search of destiny
We shall celebrate daily, weekly, monthly
and annually because we are our own anniversary!

I Miss You

I miss the sound of your voice,
the way you look at me
after I compliment you,
I just want to be
the cause of your smile
I don't expect much,
but just to be near you
when the sun goes down
and the moon comes up
My heart can be your sky,
because you are forever my star...

Push on Through

You are my escape...
Some days I'm unable to awaken
from the struggles of my life,
the demands of my dreams and my heart's desires
Sometimes it becomes a bit too overwhelming
and my mind tends to want to give up...
but I push on through
I try to get high off of my own
imagination and run free from my pains
But I see no permanent escape...
just a temporary stroll
to clear my tribulations and
lie in the place
that gives me joy
I need you...

"We Need To Talk"

Please just hear me out
and let me speak without any
interruptions of your words or thoughts
FIRST…this is my eulogy to a love
that we once sweetly embraced
and danced in wholeheartedly
I have given it my whole, but its
selfishness has corrupted my own happiness
and kept me unhappy
SECOND…please forgive me
for probably breaking your heart
and suddenly departing, yet it was inevitable
But you and I both know that this
separation is far from sudden…
In this relationship I have deposited my heart,
my mind, my dreams, my hopes,
But it has bankrupted me,
so I have nothing left to give,
for I have been broken and
I am now unable to go on
It may pain us both to depart,
but the choices of the heart
are always the most difficult to make
THIRD…we can not remain friends
because I refuse to confuse my present
with my past…as I have realized that
you are no longer my future
I know you may hate me,
burn my name with hurtful words to your friends,
devalue what we once had
But I am strong enough to embrace the criticism that
I have been preparing myself for
As we both know that the time would
eventually arrive for us to part ways
LAST…I know you may attempt to
change my mind, when it is your turn to speak,
as you try to convince me to give it another try…
but history and heartaches are all that I
have left in me…for us
So I end this by giving you the floor to speak,
but please choose your words wisely
because I have finally been awaken!

Fearless

I am not one to be afraid of taking chances
and I don't claim to know what you want nor
what you need...but hear me out
I just want to celebrate your smile and offer
you something different than
what you've been used to
I'm not going to make any promises
or paint you hopes of what could be
I just want to be near you and
Hopefully help you get to
the blessing of your talent
Just be real with me,
give me a reason to trust you,
respect you, fight for you...
than maybe we can move on
and talk about this possibility!

King

He saw her,
her torch gave
light to the
tunnels that he
always dwelled in,
she became his
bright light.

Queen

She spoke with
confidence,
for she knew
her reputation
preceded her,
and her King
admired from
the audience.

Deception (me)

Under this illusion,
I have falsely given you my smiles
and in return I have hidden my cowardice ways
I have long yearned for your touch,
dreamed about quiet conversations under the moon
Envisioned you and I traveling the world
and experiencing God's beautiful earth
I have already thanked you,
in front of many crowds for inspiring me
At night...I replay our conversations
and pray for your safe journeys,
as I anxiously anticipate our next encounter
Maybe it is a bit selfish of me
to love you secretly
and clothe it under just a friendship,
that has come to define our bond to the world
But at times, we must accept
the roads paved before us and travel them,
because we know not what light lies ahead
All things have their time and patience
brings forth what we need,
rather than what we just want
So in the mean time,
I will continue to give you my love
and steal pieces of yours
To me, it is what will cement
our connection, but to you...
it may be the worst form of deception!

What We Have

What we have,
people search their
entire lives to find
Our conversations
are pure, genuine,
passionate and fulfilling
You have always been my
weakness, the one who
makes me smile...at any
given time or day
You are easy to love,
hard to figure out,
full of dreams,
filled with scars,
yet beautiful and
intelligent in every
way imaginable!

Forgive Me

Forgive me for my pride...
It has crippled me, kept me
from giving you all of me
I was too afraid to make
a fool out of myself, at the
same time making me
foolish enough to lose you
This pride has kept me
from my dreams and from
asking for much needed help
These words of mine are genuine,
and backed by real actions
I just want to offer you
loyalty, daily stability and
at the same time giving you
my truth and love consistently,
because pride will no longer
come between our unity

Deception (you)

This is the worst form of deception...
Meeting and sharing my life with you,
always made me feel as if there was no other
way to experience what it is to be alive
I gave you all that my heart
had to offer, as you and I
lived in the greatest moment
But your ways became selfish as I
no longer saw the potential in you
Your light began to dim,
as my feelings strayed onto other shores
Leaving me in an ocean of confusion,
yet I continued to offer you
all that I had within me
I was unable to awaken from
this love, that had gripped me, molded me,
given me tears of joy,
but equally turned around and
scolded me, deserted me,
left me to question my own loyalty
But I realized that I had begun
to create my own secrets,
in order to shield myself from
the pains and struggles,
that caused me to fight a war
within my own mind
At the end, I came to the conclusion
that you were my quiet storm,
raining down on my happiness...
You became the disruption to my world
with your untimely form of deception!

Selfish

In this dark hour, I am unable to
pacify your emotional instability
Perhaps I am the reasoning behind your past
heartbreaks that have begun to resurface
I am unable to fully reveal my inner self...
so I am to blame for your tearful pleads
I am my own worst enemy,
a coward at best for awakening your love
and not giving you what I promised
I constantly caressed your spirit
with sweet words of infinity...
even though I have already seen our demise
But is it fair to end it now,
hurt you without any malicious intent,
or await your departure
as the pain will eventually drag on
I am ashamed for what my
transgressions did to your heart
and my inability to fulfill my promises to you
So I plead for your forgiveness,
for I never intended to stain
your beautiful soul with my ways...
that have become purely
unacceptable and selfish!

Up & Down

Love can be painful at times
And all who've been scorned will agree
I only gave up a small piece of my heart
Because I always lived with that fear
Constantly questioning God's promises
Settling for unfulfilling connections
I lost my way and accepted mediocrity
So I blamed others for my struggles
Never owning up for personal mistakes
I ignored my own mirrored reflection
I was fearful of whom I had become
I knew a change was inevitable
Love had to tug at my soul
For me to find something incredible
I had to change my ways of thinking
In order to walk in God's light!

Now read this again…from the BOTTOM line to the TOP line

Chased or Kept?

You want to be chased,
but you refuse to be kept
You want a key to come and go,
but you're too impatient
to unlock a wounded heart
Sometimes you pass up a good
thing...because you're so used
to playing childish games
Just remember this...what
your 'past' did to you,
has nothing to do with the
'presence' that is offered to you,
so stop speaking of a joint 'future'
But like anything else that
is fresh in the beginning...there's
always an expiration date!

Image

Image is nothing...
The perfection of the world has never
included me in its masterpiece
See, I accept no labels
because I have no color,
nor do I subscribe to any religion,
or to any certain way of life
I only attempt to love
and show how peace
can bring about smiles
in any situation or circumstance
So if YOU were to hear my name
being spoken in any form of negativity,
I suggest that you reach for your own wisdom,
then go beyond your weakness,
and look within yourself...
For only then can you see the truth
that lies in your own heart
and realize that we are all in search of LOVE,
regardless of the images
that THEY,
or better yet WE,
paint of ourselves and of others...

Forever

I want to dance with you,
lights off, music on,
but not too loud though
because I need to hear your
heartbeat next to mine
I want to feel your soft hands
caressing the back of my neck
Your lips brushing against the side of
my face as chills roll down my body
I want to hold you near me, so you know that I need you
I want to look into your eyes slowly,
patiently, so you can see
the genuine love that I have for you
I want you to know that I care for you and always
know that your happiness is important to me
I want to have a life long friendship with you,
so you always feel safe with me
I want you to place
your fears in my responsibility
I want to take my time when I kiss you,
so we can enjoy the joy of love
What an illusive word and emotion love is…
I want to take care of you,
and I want you to take care of me
I want be vulnerable with you
and place my trust in you
I want to play with your hair,
as you fall asleep on my chest
Handle your heart with ease,
introduce you as my better half,
and always stare and admire you from a far
I want us to live in each other's space,
meet at love's pace…knowing
that what we have, is what WE have,
and it has no description
But forgive me for rambling on…
So please…tell me what do you want?

Honesty

Where would we be without honesty…
I offer you my reality,
my credibility, my vulnerability and this
unshaken loyalty, until you
no longer want to stand beside me
I would rather you
break me with your truths
than shatter me with endless lies
But this honesty pains me at times
because it pains you…
I never want to be afraid
to open up to you
and in response you leave me with
your own fears of love
I want you to be bold
and smear me with your dreams,
for only then will I love you evermore
I want to think about you
in the dark because your smiles
gives me God's light
I need you to know that
I love this friendship of ours
You have given me
what most people lack…
and that is genuine honesty!

I am afraid to admit It

What if I were to tell you how
you make me feel?
Every chance I get...I steal
pieces of your smile
I'm addicted to your laughter
and the happiness in you
I just want to live in your joy,
be the reason for you to love
I become childishly happy when you
come to mind...you make me shy
There's no time quite like when we
hug and I'm taken by your aroma
I pray to always remain in your
state of ecstasy...you are my drug
Sometimes I wonder what if...
other times I'm just to afraid to admit it!

Beautiful

In my lifetime, I have never come across
anyone who gives me endless peace,
gives me the true passion of love,
and most importantly, gives me hope in this life
Your patient words have taught me
how to listen and how to apply this heart of mine
Your infinite zeal for perfection
teaches me how to write with purpose,
how to speak with conviction,
how to act with vision
You give me what you also give to the world,
but I embrace your words personally,
embody them and make them part of me
Thanking you would be an understatement,
because it would never show you
the right portrait of what you
will forever mean to my life
You are a person of inspiring potential,
as I stand in a crowd of admirers,
watching you *M.C.* the stage
Giving us all a piece of your inner beauty,
sharing your life experiences
and offering your future plans
to help the world regain
its humanity, its morality...its love
You are a rare, unique and complex being,
a teacher of sorts, a genuine soul,
a peaceful angel, a spirit
who embodies the true definition
of what it is to be beautiful!

Vulnerable

I have come to realize that I
can't trust myself around you...
I'm weak when you're near,
and my guard goes down as I have
no fear of being myself around you
But I'm careful with my words,
careful not to push you away
I'm vulnerable and free
when we're together
I guess I just want to say
that pride means nothing
when it comes to you
I just want this feeling to
forever be in our presence
I want to live in this world with
you beside me...always!

One & Only

You are my one and only...
These words will never fully
describe how you move me
I will give you my last breath and
my beating heart...if someone
ever breaks yours
If you need my comfort,
I will always be close by
If you need someone to dance with,
or a word of encouragement,
you can always find me
I offer you the kindest smiles
and the most gentle words
What you have
given me...is God sent
You believed in me,
made me feel worthy,
in the face of adversity
Wish I knew what made you
see the beauty in me
Everything that He blesses me
with...I share with you
You are my one and only!

One Night

If I can hold you for one night,
show you how much I adore you
These words of mine could
never show you how beautiful
you have always been to me
There were times that I felt
like I was not going to make it
But you gave me strength
and endless encouragement,
You supported my struggle,
believed in my dream,
and made me feel good
I am forever grateful to you,
and that beautiful heart of yours
I adore you...

Numb

I was reborn in your storm…
drenched by your distant love
that is fearful of my heart
But how can I offer you more
if you see me in the same light as
those who came before me?
I nervously plead with you to
not let this opportunity surpass us…
foregoing this chance to dance a
lifetime together in the night, as we
become the world's light
At times I smile at the future
that you and I have begun to build
Endlessly waited for you in my dreams
as I have always felt your heart beating for me…
yet I had never seen your face in the light

Bare With Me

I hope it is ok to ask…
But I want you to hear me out
and do some things for me
I want you to call me whenever
I cross your mind…with no hesitation
I hope that you will tell me your heart,
and let me show you what true love is
I want you to hold my hand,
trust in me, relay your every doubt to me
Maybe we can walk together,
kiss when we feel the desire to,
and never plan out what is to be
I want you to show me
what your heart feels for me,
and never hide anything that
you believe will ever hurt me
I need you to look into my eyes
and never lie to me,
be truthful regardless
of the unknown outcome
I know sometimes I am hardheaded,
so I ask you to be patient with me
I hope that I do not ask too much of you,
but I just want to know if you can
do these things for me and hopefully bare with me…

Right Now

Here at this time,
at this precise moment,
I have come to realize
that I need you to no end
I want to give you
every piece of this love
that I have within me
I don't want to waste another
minute away from you
I want to dance with you,
laugh with you,
grow old with you,
connect my soul to your spirit
I need you to be my peace,
my place of love,
my house of comfort
I don't want to live another day
without you beside me
You are needed now
and for as long as we can be...

Wasting Our Time?

If I am not afraid to lose you,
If I don't get excited when we speak,
If I don't smile when I see you,
If I don't imagine your scent,
If I don't softly caress your face,
If I don't wish to kiss you slow,
If I don't yearn for your presence,
If I don't run my fingers through your hair
If I am not always thinking of you,
If I never make time to see you,
If I don't feel liberated with you,
If you don't make my heart happy,
If you don't inspire me to be better...
then we are both wasting our most
precious possession...our time!

Out of Order

In the beginning I was innocent…
blind to the emotions of my heart
This was a young love
that came and embodied me,
shielding me from the world's pain
But the gripping fear of pain and the experience
of being hurt, no longer allowed
me to step out of my comfort zone
I closed off my heart to potential suitors,
only allowing casual encounters,
and remaining skeptical of their personal intentions
But you arrived as a beautiful breeze,
easily grazing me with your calculated words
Putting my mind at ease
as your smiles began to unlock my shackles
You removed my reservations with ease
as I slowly began to trust in you
My fear inevitably and slowly faded,
as the sign outside the door to my soul
had been changed by your light
For you became the reasoning behind my joy,
yet I expected nothing from you
So I am now comforted with your loyalty,
at peace with our reality
and thankful that you became
the cause for my heart being
no longer out of order…

You (again)

In a room full of people,
there is admiration,
compliments and adoration
I glance out onto the crowd, just
to see you smiling up at me
Their applause...honors me,
but your heart humbles me
"They" say that this road is hard
and arduous...but I know that all is
possible if you are beside me
So many praise my work,
and I am thankful...but YOU
are my daily inspiration
When so many are screaming
for my attention...I stop, give thanks,
and remember your positive whispers
in this room full of people!

Hope

I can now base my happiness on hope…
Sometimes I find myself smiling,
pleasantly wishing to hear your voice
I only desire to make you happy,
be your light in every dark day
I want to watch you succeed,
as your dreams inevitably come to pass
I wish to lie next to you,
hold you through the night
as your fears are tenderly relieved
I kindly ask you,
to place your needs in my hands,
allow me to show you what
love really entails
For in time I can be your guide,
effortlessly helping you
in your pilgrimage to a land of happiness
I know it may seem far fetched,
but I have now based
my life on this one simple hope…

Let's be Realistic

It is easy to paint pictures
of living happily in love
Tell you how I can
give you joy like no other
Reveal my heart to you so
the entire world can envy you
Show you what love is
supposed to be and what
patience can bring you
I can tell you how I
want to kiss you slowly
and dance with you until
we create our own rhythm
Or how we can walk this earth
together and be an
example for all others
to gracefully follow
I can promise you many
things and always keep my word
But…this is not what I
want for you or I
I want to see you grow
and achieve your dreams
Help you along the way,
and even give you
words of advice if needed
I just want to be there
when you reach your happiness
and accomplish your goals
Then we can joke about the
struggles of life,
the beauty of friendship
and the privilege of
watching each other grow in love!

Hesitant

...I know you're
hesitant to love again,
so I'm not here to
promise you anything
We've both been hurt,
so we're both guarded
and afraid to open up
So can we take this
one day at a time?
I just want the opportunity
to show you how
easy love could be
I want you to know that I
need you more than the
world will ever know...

Untitled

Inside the loudest sound that
I have ever heard,
you whispered life into me
I was lost within the sound of silence
You gave me the greatest gift,
one that no one had ever offered me
…HOPE…
Sometimes we believe in ourselves,
then equally lose ourselves
But you offered me kind words,
sweet smiles and peace in your eyes
Our childish behavior
brought about our greatest happiness
As you breathed reality into my dreams
and expected nothing in return
Always perfecting your approach
without the slightest effort
We were bonded in our words,
while honeymooning in our laughter
I photocopied your joy in my mind
and forever promised myself
to return it back to you,
…but I have yet to keep my word…
You inspired me and taught me
what the beauty of patience entailed
We never pressured our situation,
we just enjoyed each other's company
and left our connection untitled…

Celebrate

Every single day of this life,
I celebrate our connection
I know that it may be too much to
ask for your partnership in eternity
So we will just deal with this
loving reality that we have

I no longer dream of you,
for you are forever beside me
The world knows the depth
of my adoration and how
you have become my weakness
Therefore I celebrate you
through every line, every word,
every encounter that we retain
I want to scream it to the skies,
so there is no misconception
of the one that completes me

I ask, not to trouble you,
but to only make you smile,
for us to always celebrate this bond
that we have been given
I only pray that you will always
compliment me,
walk beside me,
support me,
because I intend to
passionately celebrate you…

Why I Love You

I love you.
Not because you are kind to me
or because you help me
in any way
I love you because I see
the beauty in
your soul, the potential of
your heart,
the wisdom in your face
I don't mean
to scare you or push you away,
I just wanted to reveal
this truth to you
I love you because you make
me smile, you give me
insight, you give me time in
your precious schedule
I love you
because you take your time
to laugh and share your life with me
I tell you that I love you
because this is the only feeling
that I can describe to you
I love you because you
are a true friend
to me and you help me grow daily

Being Heartbroken

Heartbroken…
I have known no greater pain!
Offering your joy to
someone without expecting
anything in return, but respect
Sometimes we lose ourselves,
going from smiles, kisses,
eye stares, to tears,
unanswered questions,
breakdowns, insecurities,
misplaced blame
Mistrust and concealment
of the heart lead to fear…
that keeps us all
from loving freely
But you must rise and
never allow your past heartbreak
to determine your future…

Compliment

I just want to compliment you!
Tell you how much I
love your smile
The way you look at me
makes me feel special
Your kisses cause me to
reevaluate my life
But we stand on different
shores, looking at opposite
sunrises and sunsets
So how can we ever lie in
each other's peace?
For the pieces around us
do not fit us perfectly
So walk away, forget
my voice, and how
I held and kissed you,
but forever keep a place in
your heart for me…

After it All

After the applause stops,
the accolades disappear,
the praise cease to exist,
the tears flow with joy…
this becomes reality
After we shed our tears,
stare at each other's souls,
surpass everyone's opinion…
The moment presents itself,
and time becomes our
greatest asset, then…
only then will I know that
it is about just
you and I!

Us

We have it all...
this is based on joy and pain.
We argue, make up,
say our apologies
and hold hands again
Never afraid to be vulnerable
with one another
Many speak on our situation,
but they have no idea
as to how much I adore you
So why worry about
anything or anyone,
because if it is meant to be,
love will eventually
pave the way...

Fate

I was left pleading, stranded alone,
riddled with misery
at the edge of hopelessness
Fate finally caught up
with me, in an uncomfortable state
It stained me, shamed me,
completely overtook me,
without a greeting or a farewell
But its residue was spread
throughout my frame,
discoloring my being,
leaving me with no identity
So when the tears came,
I pleaded to have its name...
I figured at least I
deserved that for peace
of mind and healing
But it scattered itself on my body,
before scarring my confusion with
happiness and sadness
Leaving with no response
to my lonely pleads
But in the far whispers,
I yelled out LOVE...
please come back!

-WAR-

Realization

I've come to realize that I
can't make everyone happy
No matter what I write,
treat people kindly and do for others,
there will always be a naysayer
Worrying about what others say,
will only dim my daily light and
slow down my walk in life
As you read this and shake your
head with agreement, someone
else is reading it with
discontentment in their heart
But I smile towards them and
offer them the joy that God
taught me to walk and speak with
I have chosen to keep my focus on
this journey, offering love along
the beautiful path called life,
because if I stop to address
everyone who doesn't wish me
well or has something negative to
say about me...I will only stifle my
own growth, limit my talent and
most importantly...delay my blessings!

For Nelson Mandela

Sitting here in the dark, tears rolling
down my face, I've come to realize
that time is the most precious
commodity on this earth
Today I promise myself to be
more forgiving, considerate,
kind and loving to others
Be more efficient in my writing,
because the world needs it
No more excuses, because there
are people who do more with less
I want my life to be a shining example
of nothing but love and peace for all
I pledge my allegiance to
humanity and offer my service
for the betterment of all people
The world's happiness will
indeed bring me hope and joy...

Silently they claim to trust in God
These same whispers were heard as *President James Polk*
stole the west coast lands from *Mexico*
Democracy must prevail, as they stated in the overthrow of the
government of *Haiti* and then occupy it for over 19 years
Fears are heard by all Cubans as Batista is placed in power,
but only to be overthrown by the U.S.
supported infamous revolutionary named *Fidel Castro*
In God they trust as *Jacobo Arbenz* is killed in *Guatemala*
and *Salvador Allende* is murdered in *Chile*,
in order for *Augusto Pinochet* to become the newly appointed
president by the North American government
In God they trust, I say in God they trust as the
Mujahideen and *Osama bin Laden* are armed and
trained to fight the Russians and keep power in *Afghanistan*
In God they trust but to only help
Saddam Hussein's Baath Party kill President *Abdul Qassim*
and take control of Iraq
But at the same time, they trust in God as they
support the dictatorships of *Pol Pot* in *Cambodia*,
Jonas Savimbi in *Angola* and fervently train
the *Bolivian Army* to hunt down and kill
the famous revolutionary known to all as *Ernesto "Che" Guevara*
In God they trust, I say this out loud with the flag in hand,
never forgetting how they supported the
racist *South African* apartheid government that killed *Steve Biko*
and imprisoned *Nelson Mandela* for 27 years
In God they trust, to help them iron out their conscience
for putting *Joseph Mobutu* in power in the *Congo*,
as they orchestrated the assassination of *Patrice Lumumba*
In God they trust, to help hide the truth
behind their assistance to the *Portuguese* government
in the killing of Cape Verde's *Amilcar Cabral*
In God they trust, that we never find out how they helped
those "brothers" in the killing of *Malcolm X* or
how they ended the life of *Dr. King*…then commemorated him
Oh this is a nation that strongly trusts that God
will help them erase the truth behind the murder of
Filiberto Ojeda Rios in *Puerto Rico,*
Walter Rodney in *Guyana* and how they exposed
Dr. Pedro Albizu Campos to radiation in their prisons
They may try to wash away the blood off their hands,
but God has made us well aware of their actions…
so I wonder in what god do they trust?

Defamation of Religion

I have embodied all that religion
has shown mankind through history
In me, you will find the defamation of all
human characters and sectors
Layers of skin colors,
which have aligned their souls
with the pitfalls of hell
In the beginning, greed led me
to enslave the Black, Brown & Red man,
through the justifications of Ephesians 6:5
But I would strive to blaze all
paths with my ambitious and religious desires
Fires would flow through my eyes
as my Christian brothers would
terrorize and lynch in the name of Christ
For I despised all whom were not
of the *master race* and destroyed the Jewish
peasants at a steady pace
I have risen as many characters and
defamed many religious organizations
Thus, I now kill in His name,
even though I greet you in the Name of Peace
No longer am I at ease with this lost conscience of mine;
therefore I will soon cease to exist…

(*Outlining the history of Evil Men of All Colors & Creeds*)

Politics As Usual

Within the cloudy rumors or war,
we see the simple rhetoric
of condescending old political men
Men who believe that their earthly
knowledge is aligned with the wisdom
of the omnipotent Father
But their thoughts are weak
and their actions reflect the simplicity
of what man has the ability to do
Yet in the midst of their confusion,
young men offer their lives,
in return for mournful mothers
and heart-broken fathers
For it is within the politics of rich and aging men,
that we find the true
essence of war and the burning
desires of what has scorched the earth
But with every death, there's a birth
thus mankind shall continue
to negotiate the tender prices of innocent lives,
for the gains of immorality and currency
So when will they embrace humility
and finally practice the true
doctrines of democracy?

Do Better

You must do better than your best!
You must reject all negativity
that doesn't align with your spirit
and tries to distract you from
the beauty of your dreams
You must be aware of your
emotions and never be
overcome with imbalance
Your mind and heart must
always remain on the same path
and shun the propaganda of war
Everyday your compassion must
be measured for progress
You must always be honest
and transparent with yourself
You must be consistent in practicing
discipline within your own personal war and on your
road to self exploration and success!

Scars

Pieces of me are scattered
everywhere
Many nights I cried
when no one could see,
too ashamed of my own struggles
I was emotionally scarred
fighting endless internal wars
from the beatings of my life
I was unable to love without
detaching from the chains of fear
So how can I offer you my heart, if the
ruins are buried beneath this pain
But you give me hope, you give me joy,
you give everything that will
always keep me sane...and
that is true love to me
So now I proudly embrace these
scars of mine...unashamed and
proud to stand for anyone in need!

No Time

The problem is that
you think
you have time
as war is on the horizon

Stop assuming
that people will put up
with empty promises

Time is to be cherished...
not toyed with
So stop taking people for granted

Forgive while you still
have time, in order to relieve that
burden from your heart
Work on reaching those dreams,
because father time waits for no one!

It is your Life

Never live to please others
nor for the opinion of society
Sometimes caring too much
can be your downfall
Remember that not everyone is
happy to see you succeed
Most are fighting their
own demons and emotional wars
So open your eyes,
learn to protect your heart,
love with no bitterness,
focus on your dreams,
smile often as you cry less,
forgive for your peace of mind,
but never be a fool twice...

Break

Building a world of simplicity,
has come with an enormous
price of many lost lives
Humanity now reaps the sins
sowed by our predecessors,
therefore our prayers are endless
We fight *within*, in order
to keep the *without* from shattering
Men and women who give way to
the whispers of the mind,
and then lead nations to war blindly
Silently, we state our opposition,
yet fears overwhelm our flesh,
as we allow our lives to rest in their hands
Races begin to separate through
false ideology and through various
opposing religious manifestations
For we have fallen apart and
allowed the covenant of
man and God to finally break…

Warmongers

No longer am I at ease with
the false promises of men
Men of war who offer peace and freedom
in return for the lives of young boys
Boys who are to never see
the light of their dreams or the smiles
of their loving families and friends
Yet we remain at ease with their foreign policies,
which are to soon bring war
to our vulnerable seas
But they only see the currency
that comes from occupying other states
and other societies
For we speak our peace
in the presence of our peers,
yet fear consumes us
when we see our false leaders
Leaders who have misled our image for years
and stained our characters
throughout all of this world's borders

Murderers

These streets have been paved by murderers,
violently painting our walk ways with anger
Spewing their pains of poverty and neglect all over
innocent bystanders and illegal money handlers
Preachers fear their own doorsteps,
so they remain within church halls…where safety is assumed
But our lives are being consumed by
profiling police orders, who are bred with
rage towards our lost children
Age is not a factor when these political
murderers take aim at our communities,
riddling our neighborhoods with false hope
Life's meaning is now *meaningless*
as our sons light the candles of retaliation,
and our daughters contemplate lives
of unscrupulous occupations
Fathers become cellmates with uncles
as their forgotten wives suffer in darkness of
unwanted fondles as drugs penetrate in bundles
But everyone cries in silence as
suicides, murders and overdoses
remain our greatest hurdles
…so who is at fault…
Police are corrupt, leaders are abrupt,
parents are inept, children are a wreck
as the devil's plan has been perfected and directed
for us all to play a part in this grotesque act
So analyze and then realize
that this compromise with our lives,
has made us all living lies,
and pushed our sons and daughters
over the moral borders,
and turned them into cold hearted murderers…

-Stop The Violence-

Why I Write

I continue to write because my light
has begun to awaken some eyes
Yes my people, God does exist!
I write because I am must speak
of the powerful judgment
that is soon to come to these shores
I write for the love of Gandhi
and for the memory of Marley
I write to remind you of Mandela's patience
and for the memory of all peace seekers
I write for all people who have begun to rebel
against their nation and continue to grow more and more
impatient with political indignation against third world nations
I write for the end of violence,
because in time they will come to silence us all
I write for the sake of Amilcar Cabral
and for the courage of Toussaint L'Ouverture
I write because man sinned from the very start and
because we will forever fall short of His grace

Land of Opportunity

Mass shootings have riddled
this broken education system
Poverty affects all races as
foreclosure of many homes run rampant
This jobless economy has become
the catalyst for our high divorce rate
We are living under an unjust "justice" system
that allows killers to walk free
Politicians continually display their
contempt and disrespect
for their president
As they hypocritically vote to
sponsor the governments of Afghanistan,
Iraq, Syria and Egypt...
yet shut down the flow of
our own government
Welcome to the land of opportunity!

Hold on a bit Longer

Everyday I get a little closer to that dream,
as my weaknesses fight me a little harder
I think back to the struggling years,
the endless rejections and the hopelessness
that almost took over me. But I persevered...
because the mission was much bigger than me
Change is inevitable when the tears begin
to turn frustration to motivation.
The feeling of achieving your dream is indescribable
and hard to explain. I'm trying to hold on through faith,
but doubt endlessly attempts to end
all of the hard work that has been put forth
I have vowed to push onward, because backwards
brought me nothing but disappointment
Broken, resurrected, restored and rejuvenated,
yet through it all I remained faithful to my dream
I will continue on as I look forward
to claiming my deliverance and fulfilling the promise,
that was placed within me. Giving up is not an option...
for everyday I get a little closer to achieving
what I was put on this earth to do!

Conviction

I pull at my conscience for that
ever so silent voice of God,
in order to give way to my joys
But it continues to elude me and
tempt me at an equal time
But how is this so?
Maybe the hearts that I have broken
in the past, have come to taste
revenge in my present pains
For they say that it only comes through
loneliness...revenge that is!
But I wonder if my short-comings,
will become my convictions in time
It matters not,
because at the end of it all,
only my mirrored dreams
will reflect in the dark...

President vs God

PRESIDENT
gave the order,
as victory came
with a price for
the souls that
HE was responsible
for sending and losing
His nation rejoiced,
he battled his conscience,
for HIS spirit reminded
him that one day he
would have to
answer to
GOD

Just Words

Their words should mean nothing to you
and the life that you have chosen to live
They are always
going to gossip about you,
spread rumors about
you and try to derail your progress...
and it's only because you
no longer pay them any mind
What they say about YOU,
only affects THEM because
they are hurting within
So pray for them,
ask God to guide them and
put love in their hearts
See, we were all put here to do
great things in God's name
Remember that you were
ignorant and lost once,
but now you have seen His Word
So it is your duty
to help them reach that light...
because you were given
vision for a reason!
So teach as your Father above
has delivered you, saved you,
guided you and taught you

Road to Success

Not everyone is going to understand your
dream, nor your sacrifices or
even your limited time to socialize
Your struggle is going to be lonely
sometimes, even heartbreaking
But it's meant to open up your
eyes and see who will be there
for the long run
I know you will be hurt,
tearful and even mad
But it's all in the plan that God
created for you to be exactly
where you need to be, in
order to receive your
blessing
I know it seems far and
unreachable,
but with every day,
every experience and
every lesson that you
receive...you get a bit closer!

Expired Dreams

Everything has its time…
I'm thankful and grateful for
everyone who has come into my
life and played a part in making me
the person that I am today
But sadly nothing lasts forever,
so friendships will fade,
relationships will end...
but hopefully none are bitterly departed
It is part of life,
so I don't dwell much on what ended,
but rather on the lessons learned
Growth only comes from accepting what was
and not what I wanted it to be
So go in peace, reach your dreams,
find success and hopefully
one day we will cross paths again.

Life, Love & War

...Life is about experiences...
Love can be tricky,
even painful to some, if we tend to
give too much of our hearts
But we fight our war with no regrets,
knowing that what we offer
is pure, genuine and real
We shun war, even if
we are prosecuted for treason
Some may never appreciate
what we offer them,
but we continue to live on,
and never allow bitterness
to overcome our happiness
So smile, be proud of the
beauty in your spirit
and what you offered this earth
Your generosity will eventually
overflow, giving your soul,
body and spirit...the happiness,
peace and love that you deserve!

Made in the USA
Middletown, DE
09 January 2015